THE N

THE NEIGHBOUR

A play by

Meredith Oakes

For Tom

6

First published in 1993 by Oberon Books Limited
521 Caledonian Road
London N7 9RH
Tel: 071 607 3637 * Fax 071 607 3629

ISBN 1 870259 31 9

Printed by The Longdunn Press, Bristol
Cover illustration by Peter Farmer
Cover design by Lorraine Hodghton
Back cover photo by Mark Douet

OBERON BOOKS LIMITED
Managing Director: Charles Glanville
Publishing Director: James Hogan
Associate Editor: Nicholas Dromgoole MA [Oxon], FIChor

The Neighbour was commissioned by the Royal National Theatre Studio, where workshop presentations were given on 28th and 29th August, 1992, with the following cast:

Margaret	Mary Macleod
John	Ben Chaplin
James	Lee Ross
Stephi	Emma Amos
Liz	Flaminia Cinque
Michael	Jamie Hinde
Sheila	Liz Fraser
Reg	Michael Beint

The first public performance was given at the Royal National Theatre, Cottesloe auditorium on 21st April, 1993, as part of the Springboards Festival with the following cast:

Margaret	Mary Macleod
John	Ben Chaplin
James	Lee Ross
Stephi	Clare Holman
Liz	Flaminia Cinque
Michael	Jonny Lee Miller
Sheila	Vilma Hollingbery
Reg	Michael Beint

Both productions were directed by John Burgess and designed by Jackie Brooks.

Characters

John, *a young man*
Margaret, *his mother*
Stephi, *a young woman*
James, *the young man she lives with*
Liz, *James' sister*
Sheila, *a woman in her fifties*
Reg, *Sheila's husband*
Michael, *a young man, James' friend*

Also the offstage voice of Celestine

Time: 1990s. Setting: a London council estate.

ACT ONE

Scene 1

Outside John's council flat. A summer evening.
[JOHN is putting something in the dustbin. MARGARET, his mother, comes out]
MARGARET: Are you off out?
JOHN: No.
MARGARET: I thought you was off out.
JOHN: No.
MARGARET: Are you coming in then?
JOHN: In a minute.
MARGARET: What you want to stay out here for?
JOHN: I got a life to lead. Watch out for the door.
[The door is swinging closed]
MARGARET: *[Stopping the door from closing]* Got a key, have
    you?
JOHN: No.
MARGARET: Neither do I.
JOHN: Don't shut it then.
MARGARET: Are you coming in?
JOHN: Yes, I'm coming in now.
MARGARET: All right. *[She goes in shutting door behind her]*
JOHN: Mum! *[Sotto voce]* Fucking vegetable. *[Bangs on the door]*
    Mum! *[Gives up, turns away from the door]* It's a beautiful
    summer night. You can hear the weeds growing. They're
    making fertile use of restricted space, like the rest of us. This
    estate won a design award for witty, compact provision. We've
    got a red toilet seat. The place is a blank to me. Unreal. No
    shelter. I believe it was completed five years ago. Before that,
    the weeds had all the space they wanted. Now they're fighting
    it out in two hundred garden plots, each the size of a grave but
    less nourishing. I don't feel lonely out here. In there with her
    I feel lonely. But I mean to make this my home. The superior
    man creates, by his very existence, a place of safety.
[JAMES bursts out of the next door house, pursued by STEPHI]
JAMES: Get off.

STEPHI: No.

JAMES: Mind my sleeve.

STEPHI: If you go, I'm going back in and cut your clothes to pieces.

JAMES: If you do, I'll get the law on you.

STEPHI: Come back.

JAMES: What for?

STEPHI: I never meant what I said.

JAMES: What you say it for?

STEPHI: I said it to upset you.

JAMES: Yes well it does upset me.

STEPHI: You ain't what I said.

JAMES: Maybe I am.

STEPHI: You ain't.

JAMES: We'll see what I am. We'll see who's the fucking loser. You're the fucking loser. How much you make in a day?

STEPHI: Come inside.

JAMES: You make fuck-all. You work your fucking arse off cleaning up after skinflint fucking yuppies and you make fuck-all, so who are you calling a fucking loser?

STEPHI: Before I'd be what you are, I'd clean sewers.

JAMES: That's how you see me ain't it. Clean fucking sewers. Lick the fuckers clean if you want.

STEPHI: I didn't mean it. I never meant it. It's my temper James.

JAMES: Piss off.

STEPHI: Come back in. Come in eh.

JAMES: What you want a fucking loser for?

STEPHI: Come in. [*A car horn sounds. They look towards it*] Bitch.

JAMES: [*Calling*] New motor.

CELESTINE: [*Off*] I come to take you for a ride.

STEPHI: Where did she get that.

JAMES: Ask her. Maybe she got it off the DHSS.

CELESTINE: [*Off*] Are you coming?

JAMES: [*To STEPHI*] Want a ride?

STEPHI: I'd sooner eat nails.

JAMES: Suit yourself. [*To CELESTINE*] Can I drive?

CELESTINE: [*Off*] Show us your licence.

JAMES: [*Puts his hand in his pocket*] I got it in here. [*To STEPHI*] See you in a minute.

STEPHI: [*As he goes*] Run it into a wall why don't you.

[*JOHN has been trying not to intrude*]

JOHN: Sorry to intrude.

STEPHI: You're welcome.

JOHN: My mum locked me out. Nice to meet you.

STEPHI: Why has it got to be him eh. Why not someone that's got a heart. The point is, I'm a pessimist. He represents my views on life. Settled in all right have you.

JOHN: Yes, we're busy settling in. My mum's a bit confused but aren't we all. Name's John.

STEPHI: Stephanie. Nice meeting you. [*She is about to go in*]

JOHN: Them newsagents, do you find them obliging?

STEPHI: They'll sell you a paper.

JOHN: Yes I thought they seemed friendly enough. Three of you is there?

STEPHI: That's right.

JOHN: You and him, you got my mum all agog. She's been listening to you fighting through the wall.

STEPHI: I expect you've been having a listen in as well.

JOHN: These walls are paper thin. Shelving is out of the question.

[*MARGARET opens the door*]

MARGARET: Where you been? I been looking all over for you.

STEPHI: [*To JOHN*] Be seeing you.

MARGARET: Wait a minute, girl, what's your name?

STEPHI: Stephanie.

MARGARET: [*To JOHN*] Ask her if she wants a cup of tea.

STEPHI: No, it's all right thanks.

MARGARET: [*To JOHN*] Is she a friend of yours?

JOHN: Yes, we're old friends.

MARGARET: You ought to bring her indoors.

STEPHI: I was just going, thanks all the same.

MARGARET: We ain't been here long.

STEPHI: No.

MARGARET: Nice to get to know people, ain't it. Some people.

STEPHI: Yes.

MARGARET: Not all people.

STEPHI: No.

MARGARET: Not round here.

STEPHI: No.

MARGARET: Do you come from round here?

STEPHI: That's right.

MARGARET: Where do you come from then?

STEPHI: I live next door to you.

MARGARET: Oh.

JOHN: [*To MARGARET*] So we'll be seeing quite a bit of her.

MARGARET: Yes. Very nice.

JOHN: You can have lots of talks. She can tell you everything goes on around here.

MARGARET: Thanks all the same.

JOHN: That ain't very polite.

MARGARET: Teaching manners you ain't got. [*To STEPHI*] He talks to me like dirt.

JOHN: Just winding you up, ain't I. I always wind you up.

MARGARET: [*To STEPHI*] He always winds me up. He thinks I ain't got any feelings, but I have.

STEPHI: Bound to, ain't you.

JOHN: Bound to.

MARGARET: He oughtn't to upset me, ought he, it makes me lose track.

JOHN: What I'll do, I'll make us a cup of tea.

MARGARET: Yes, I'll have a cup of tea.

JOHN: That's right. Stephanie might have a cup of tea as well, stop us misbehaving ourselves.

STEPHI: I ought to get back.

JOHN: He's out enjoying himself, ain't he.

STEPHI: I'll have a cup of tea.

MARGARET: Are you coming in then?

JOHN: Yes, we're coming in, don't shut the bleeding door on us. [*They go in*]

Scene 2

Later the same evening, inside the home of JAMES, LIZ and STEPHI.

[*LIZ is making a woollen pompom. STEPHI comes in*]

LIZ: I didn't know what to do with your toast.

STEPHI: Did James come in?

LIZ: No. I put it in the bin. Were you wanting it?

STEPHI: No.

LIZ: You could have warmed it up, couldn't you. What a shame. I hope you didn't want it.

[*STEPHI is checking the channels on the TV*]

LIZ: Where's James then?

STEPHI: He's your brother, you tell me.

LIZ: I thought you and him was off together somewhere.

STEPHI: No.

LIZ: I thought you and him would have made it up.

[*STEPHI goes and checks the answering machine, but there's nothing on it*]

LIZ: Look what I made for Eddy and Freddy. [*Holds up the pompom*]

STEPHI: Yeah.

LIZ: Do you want to see me give it them? [*Goes to the cage of Eddy and Freddy*] Hullo Freddy darling, you in your wheel are you? Oh, the little love, he's a little muscle mouse. Where's your friend? Where's Eddy? Look at him, you can see his little mind going round. Eddy? Eddy? Come and see what Liz has got. Something nice and soft for you. Who was that in the car with him? Was that Celestine was it? Oh yes, ain't you a strong little mouse, you can spin that great big wheel all by yourself. Mind you don't catch your tail, that's what happens to little boys that show off. Eddy! I don't know why Eddy won't come out. You won't see James till morning then.

STEPHI: I'd fucking better.

LIZ: He's a law unto himself though, ain't he, you'll never change him. I could never change him. I never had the slightest control. He was such a lovely-looking little boy though. Oh yes Freddy, you're a lovely-looking little boy too, you've got a lovely pink nose and it's ever so pointy. Go and get Eddy for me. Go on. [*To STEPHI*] I hope Eddy's all right. He might be sick, mightn't he. I ought to take off their roof and see what he's up to. [*STEPHI switches on the TV. LIZ takes the roof off*] Look at you, you sleepyhead. Don't you want to see what I got for you? Come on, I thought you was supposed to be nocturnal. Here, what you got there. Show Lizzie. Oh! It's a baby! It's a tiny little baby. Fancy that.

STEPHI: What?

LIZ: Eddy ain't a little boy, he's a mother.

STEPHI: So much for safe sex. [*Turns off the TV*]

LIZ: Did you ever see anything so tiny? It looks like it's made of jelly, don't it, like something from the sweet shop. It's like a jelly baby with hands.

[*LIZ is reaching into the cage*]

STEPHI: Don't touch it.

LIZ: I'm only going to put it next its mother.

STEPHI: If you touch them the mother rejects them.

LIZ: Eddy won't mind. Eddy's my baby, ain't you darling.

STEPHI: Leave them be.

LIZ: I can't, I'm too excited. Where's it gone, Eddy, where's your little baby? Look behind you, stupid thing.

[*LIZ reaches into the cage, then continues watching*]

STEPHI: When he comes through that door I'm off. I'm only waiting to see how much longer he thinks he can be.

LIZ: She's Edwina now. Oh blimey, look at that, will you.

STEPHI: What's the matter?

LIZ: She's eating it. [*STEPHI looks*] Horrible little creature! Horrible little thing! Eating it! Her own baby!

STEPHI: Put the lid on. [*She does so*]

LIZ: I shouldn't have touched them, it's against their instincts ain't it. You told me not to touch them. You mustn't disturb them, must you. That's what they say.

STEPHI: What do they know eh?

LIZ: I got what was coming to me, didn't I.

STEPHI: We all make mistakes.

LIZ: But it's unnatural, ain't it. I shan't give them that pompom now.

STEPHI: Why not?

LIZ: It'll go straight in the bin.

STEPHI: Well that should bring them to their senses.

LIZ: I suppose you'll say I'm too high strung.

[*JAMES enters*]

JAMES: [*To STEPHI*] Why didn't you come?

STEPHI: Nice ride was it.

JAMES: What you looking so suspicious for. We drove down into Kent and had a drink. Guess who come in the pub. Marvin. He's living down there with his dad. He come in with a little puppy in a plastic bag with a little blanket and a Farley's rusk, except Marvin ate the rusk.

STEPHI: And?

JAMES: Marvin likes Complan too. It was a very sweet puppy. It had big brown worried eyes, like it was meekly wondering what the fuck it done wrong to end up as Marvin's dog.

STEPHI: What else?

JAMES: And then we drove back.

STEPHI: Then what?

LIZ: I'm off to bed. [*She goes, unnoticed*]

STEPHI: What did you do?

JAMES: I told you.

STEPHI: You and her.

JAMES: We went back to her place.

[*STEPHI goes into the kitchen and comes back with a knife, while JAMES sits down*]

STEPHI: Tell me about it.

JAMES: You've really got a temper on you. We didn't go anywhere.

STEPHI: You just said you did.

JAMES: Well we didn't, all right?

STEPHI: Do you expect me to believe that?

JAMES: All right, I'm lying. What you waiting for?

STEPHI: Don't tempt me.

JAMES: You're so aggressive. I feel totally secure with you. You can murder me any time you want.

STEPHI: You never give me anything I need. You never comfort me.

JAMES: I'll comfort you. Come here.

STEPHI: No.

JAMES: Come on, I'll be getting sleepy soon.

STEPHI: [*Goes across to him*] You don't understand anything.

JAMES: I know. I'm just a bastard. [*Caressing her. They kiss*] I'd like to get you a little dog.

STEPHI: What for?

JAMES: I'd like to see it being well treated. I'd like to see you feed it. I'd like to see it chew on your fingers and lick you. Then I'd fuck you.

STEPHI: The dog mightn't like that.

JAMES: Then he'd have to get out, wouldn't he. I'd kick the little fucker out and shut the door. [*While they are embracing, JAMES speaks, unheard by STEPHI*] I know people, you only got to brush against them and money rubs off. Celestine give me twenty to get her a drink and said keep the change. I can make a hundred in a night just by sitting in the right company in the right place. I like to feel money circulating, you can float on it. You get high on it. When I got to come off it, everything frustrates me and I become restless and irritable. I got to take it out on someone because I got too much energy and I'm very touchy. Stephi always accepts whatever I do. At times that annoys me and I get encouraged to take it further. It's just my curiosity. I'm very curious, but unfortunately she's got very few secrets.

STEPHI: Oh James, what you doing to me.

JAMES: You're so beautiful. You're so delicate. Celestine's a camel beside you.

STEPHI: Is she? Am I better?

JAMES: Yes. [*Kisses her*] You like me don't you.

STEPHI: Yes.

JAMES: Why?

STEPHI: I love you.

JAMES: What for? Stop fooling around.

STEPHI: No.

JAMES: What's wrong with you Stephi?

STEPHI: Eh?

JAMES: How can you like a black rotten heart?

STEPHI: You ain't got a black rotten heart.

JAMES: You been telling me I do.

STEPHI: I never said that.

JAMES: Like when you look at me, you see this invisible stain.

STEPHI: I only criticize you because you mean too much to me.

JAMES: So what happens if I ain't bad? You might not like me then. So you're good, is what you think, but to please you I got to be a bad boy. People are strange.

STEPHI: You're the strange one. [*Kisses his chest*]

JAMES: Fuck off! What you bite me for?

STEPHI: I never.

JAMES: You bit my heart.

STEPHI: Don't be stupid, James, I never bit you at all. If I bit you, where's the mark?

JAMES: Devils leave no mark. They suck your heart out with a straw.

STEPHI: I ain't a devil.

JAMES: I never said you was.

STEPHI: What you talking about?

JAMES: Nothing.

STEPHI: Do you know what you just said?

JAMES: Let's go to bed, I'm knackered.

STEPHI: Are you all right?

JAMES: No, I told you, I'm fucking knackered.

STEPHI: The things in your mind, you ought to see a doctor.

JAMES: I don't need no doctor. You're my doctor. Any little aches
    and pains, you fix them. You're my medicine. Rest and
    medicine is what I need. Medicine in the morning eh. [*Kisses
    her*]

Scene 3

A week later, around midday.

[*MICHAEL is sitting in a tree near the road. He has a large sports
bag. JAMES walks up*]

JAMES: Mike?

MICHAEL: Hullo James.

JAMES: You're in a tree. What's the point of it Michael?

MICHAEL: Waiting for the milk float. Late, ain't it. It's a disgrace.

JAMES: Why aren't you waiting for it in your home?

MICHAEL: I couldn't rob it if I was in my home.

JAMES: Why has that tree got no leaves? You ain't hidden. You're
    visible. Ain't you got nothing better to do?

MICHAEL: No I fucking ain't.

JAMES: Go down the pub.

MICHAEL: Pub's a fucking shithole.

JAMES: Go down the shop.

MICHAEL: Shop's a fucking rip-off.

JAMES: Go and see your mum.

MICHAEL: Mum's a fucking slag.

JAMES: Go and see your sister.

MICHAEL: She's fucking with my dad.

JAMES: Planning to raid the milk float, are you? Ambush it, will
    you?

MICHAEL: I'm working it out.

JAMES: Rich pickings there.

MICHAEL: I only need the yoghurts.

JAMES: You want that fucking bifidus, don't you. It's good for
    your fucking functions.

[*MICHAEL is climbing down. He opens his sports bag and takes out a bedding plant which has been uprooted*]

JAMES: That's a pretty flower.

MICHAEL: How many of these have I got?

JAMES: I couldn't really say Michael.

MICHAEL: Forty-two.

JAMES: That's a lot, ain't it.

MICHAEL: When I get them yoghurt pots, I can plant them in and knock them out next Sunday down the market. Two fifty a piece.

JAMES: Where did you get them.

MICHAEL: I been for a walk in the park. The security down there is a joke.

JAMES: The point is, they don't envisage somebody like you.

[*SHEILA enters*]

SHEILA: It's no use giving him flowers, Michael, he'll never appreciate you the way I do. You're looking well today, the pair of you. I do like this warm weather, it's so much more modern.

JAMES: It gives me a headache. You got anything for a headache?

SHEILA: I ain't a fucking witch.

JAMES: Go on, you got everything in that bag.

SHEILA: How would you know what I got in my bag? [*She starts to search*]

JAMES: Could you get the attention of a milkman?

SHEILA: I can't even get the attention of my husband. Here you are. Open wide. [*She feeds him a pill*]

JAMES: Got any more?

SHEILA: You're like a bleeding baby bird. [*She feeds him another*]

JAMES: Could you chat him up?

SHEILA: What for?

JAMES: Michael's short of a pint, ain't you Michael.

SHEILA: Why don't I buy him one?

JAMES: No. Tacky.

MICHAEL: Wait up. Here he is.

JAMES: [*To SHEILA*] Keep him talking across the road.

SHEILA: I need the loo.

JAMES: Wriggle them hips.

[*SHEILA goes. They watch*]

JAMES: What you going to put them in?

[*MICHAEL empties the plants out of his sports bag and goes off stage to rob the milk float. Returns a moment later with the bag full of yoghurts*]

JAMES: You're an artist, man. You are so nonchalant. You walked up to that milk like a worker to his machine. You packed that up like you was being paid for it.

MICHAEL: It's fresh here.

JAMES: It's the suspense that made me fart, Michael. Reading the labels, a master stroke.

MICHAEL: I only like the pineapple. I ain't making much on this, all right?

JAMES: Three-way split. Definite.

MICHAEL: Up your arse.

[*SHEILA returns*]

SHEILA: Oh James I felt such a fool. "Where's Canford Street," I says. "You're in it," he says. End of conversation. "Oh," says I, "fancy that, what a stroke of luck". Then lo and behold he says to me, "I feel lucky too". He wants to meet me. He says I got good bones. Don't tell Reg. I wouldn't have good bones after that.

JAMES: I'm good for you, see. I take you out of yourself. I enable you to make new friends.

[*Meanwhile MICHAEL has taken off his shirt, and is putting the plants into it and tying it up*]

SHEILA: Did you manage, Michael? Good lord, what's he doing.

JAMES: [*Takes one of the flowers, breaks off the root, gives her the top*] He's collecting samples. Come on.

[*They all leave*]

Scene 4

Outside John's house the same afternoon.

[*JOHN is using stripping fluid on a piece of wooden furniture, and scraping off the old varnish*]

JOHN: Dear Stephanie. So this is love. What was I like before I met you last week? I've forgotten. I was a closed book but now I like to think I have a reader. What is the book about? Trust. If you feel differently, it is better to find out straight away, that is why I am writing you this letter. Only a fool would stay in a burning house rather than jump out the window. Only a fool would sit outside the kitchen smelling the food but never daring to eat any in case it poisons him. Since last week, I finally hope I belong in the world though up till now I have always felt like a stranger. Shit what a wank. Start again. Dear Stephanie...

[*LIZ has entered, holding a dress*]

LIZ: Excuse me. You know nail varnish, well I spilled it on this dress. I just caught sight of you from out the window, and I thought I'd come and ask you. Could you shift it?

JOHN: Pleased to meet you.

LIZ: I'm Liz.

JOHN: I don't have much experience of cosmetics.

LIZ: I rubbed it with remover but all I did was spread it. I tried methylated spirits but I might as well have been using lemonade. So then I did leave it in Coca Cola for a while. I got some petrol and poured it over, and then a friend of mine suggested I soak it overnight in a paste of sugar, salt and vinegar with a touch of cayenne, but I think they was having me on.

JOHN: The stuff I've got here, your dress might shrivel up altogether.

LIZ: Really?

JOHN: A woman come up to me, her husband had been spray painting the car but he was a bit shortsighted and pointed it at her instead. She asked me to remove it from her dress. Before I knew what was happening she'd got hold of the bottle and was dabbing it on. Next thing, her dress fell off her in rags.

LIZ: It never.

JOHN: She was running round here bollock naked not long before you came down. It's a wonder you didn't see her from your window.

LIZ: I didn't see anything like that.

JOHN: You can't have been looking properly.

LIZ: I was though. [*Pause*] The use I've had out of this dress, it wouldn't matter anyway. It's my brother, see, he wants me to smarten myself up, go out and that. That's the reason I bought it. I don't much enjoy going out. I generally get sick to my stomach when I go out.

JOHN: What does your boyfriend say about that?

LIZ: I ain't got a boyfriend.

JOHN: Go on, I don't believe you.

LIZ: I have had, but it takes getting used to, don't it. I didn't adapt to it really. He wanted to get married but I didn't think I could face it, not having my own room and that.

JOHN: No place to hide eh.

LIZ: You know James, you must have seen James, my brother, James thinks I'm not all there. I've always been the responsible one. I'm ten years older, see, I was the one that brought him up really. I never developed, he took over where I left off. It's not my fault, is it. There's no call for him to go on about it, is there.

JOHN: None at all that I can see.

LIZ: I shouldn't be talking to you, you're busy ain't you.

JOHN: I'm sorry about the dress.

LIZ: You ought to call round one of these days. See how the other half lives.

JOHN: Yes, it's always interesting, ain't it. Mind how you go now.

LIZ: Goodbye then.

JOHN: Goodbye. [*Continues to work*] Dear Stephanie. Well. A new friend. Am I demented writing to you? Please will you find a way to reassure me. [*Stops work*] So far as I can see, the person you are currently linked with stays in bed most of the day. In the evening you are generally out. Why don't you come round and see me? He won't like it if you leave him. All in all he is plainly difficult. [*Starts work*] There must definitely be satisfaction to be got out of kicking people around in the way he seems to like, but there is also satisfaction in being more careful where one puts one's feet, and in my view this is what the superior man ought to prefer. Self-restraint. However, we all have to tread on someone some time.

[*SHEILA enters, with the flower that JAMES gave her*]

SHEILA: You'll poison yourself with that. Sorry love, did I give you a shock did I? You should have seen yourself jump. I was only saying to my husband, I wonder when the new people are going to show themselves, I've hardly set eyes on them. I'm Sheila from number nineteen.

JOHN: John.

SHEILA: And what are you up to, John?

JOHN: Doing a bit of stripping.

SHEILA: It's ever such nice wood. Worn smooth. Antique is it, like me. I hate to think what you must have paid for it.

JOHN: Once this has passed through my hands I couldn't afford it. A man I know sells them see, I clean them up for him.

SHEILA: Creative. Lovely.

JOHN: Indoors with that stripping fluid it's enough to make you puke.

SHEILA: You need a nice big space with somewhere to put all your equipment. My husband works on cars at the moment, he does it up the road, I won't have him under my feet. There he is, he's just coming down. Big, ain't he. Big and wayward. Not for the faint-hearted.

[REG appears]

SHEILA: Come here and meet John.

REG: [Wiping his hands] Look at that. Blood. I must have took a piece out of my finger.

JOHN: I hope it's not serious.

REG: Ask yourself this. What is serious?

SHEILA: He once had his ear bit off in a fight and he never noticed until they saw it lying on the floor.

REG: Here. See this scar on my neck?

JOHN: My goodness yes.

REG: Four years ago I had this growth troubling me. I got sick of waiting to see them in casualty so I come home here and took it off with a chisel.

SHEILA: The doctor said he ought to have been a sculptor.

REG: Tell him how I proposed to you.

SHEILA: Propose. He never proposed. The first time I went out with him he took out this knife and cut the knickers off me.

REG: I knew straight away she was the one.

JOHN: Those were romantic days.

SHEILA: You got your mother with you, is that right?

JOHN: Yes.

SHEILA: I seen her on the doorstep talking to herself, bless her.

JOHN: That's her.

SHEILA: Change upsets them, don't it. What is it exactly? She ain't that old.

JOHN: No, not that old.

SHEILA: What a shame. What exactly do they say it is?

JOHN: Nothing definite, nothing anyone ought to put a name to. Often as not she's all right.

SHEILA: The people before you died out. [To REG] He wouldn't leave the house, would he.

REG: Never left the house.

SHEILA: She did all the to-ing and fro-ing. He never even went to her funeral.

REG: He was afraid of his own shadow. Well. Think about it. A man's own shadow is a frightening thing.

SHEILA: So we could never get close to them really. Any night you want to come in for a drink, or a Sunday afternoon you know, our door is always open.

JOHN: Thank you very much.

REG: Better go indoors and get washed up.

JOHN: That's a nasty cut.

REG: I'll crush some garlic on it, pour on a bit of vodka, soon be good as new. [*He goes*]

SHEILA: Nice to meet you.

JOHN: Mind how you go. [*She goes*] Dear Stephanie. Are they friends of yours?

Scene 5

Later the same afternoon, outside John's house. The piece of furniture is gone.

[*JAMES arrives, calling to MICHAEL who is offstage*]

JAMES: Hey Mike!

MICHAEL: What you want?

JAMES: Think it over.

MICHAEL: What?

JAMES: Three ways man!

MICHAEL: Piss off!

JAMES: All right, you and me.

MICHAEL: Dip your balls in batter!

JAMES: Watch yourself!

[*Picks up half a brick, throws it at MICHAEL who is still offstage*]

MICHAEL: Accurate throw James. [*Throws the brick back. JAMES dodges*]

JAMES: [*Throws the brick back*] Stand still you fucker!

[*MICHAEL throws the brick back. JAMES dodges and the brick goes through the glass in Margaret's front door. MARGARET emerges*]

MARGARET: You come here! [*JAMES looks towards MICHAEL but he has run away*] Did you throw that?

JAMES: No.

MARGARET: Yes you did.

JAMES: No I fucking didn't.

MARGARET: My son will be back in a minute.

JAMES: That's nice.

[*He turns to go. MARGARET catches hold of him*]

MARGARET: What about my hall? You ought to see in there. You
ought to pick that up. You ought to walk on that in your bare
feet, see what it's like for others. Who's going to fix my glass?
Anyone can get in there, it's not safe. I'm going to get the law
on you.

JAMES: I ain't done nothing, you old fungus.

MARGARET: You near frightened me out of my wits. I can't keep
track when I'm upset. They'll never fix that, will they. My son
says to me, two weeks we been here, are you happy, and I says
no, this sink's blocked, and he says, we'll get someone in to fix
it, and I says no we won't, they'll never bleeding come. They
never will.

JAMES: That's because you disgust them. I'm going now.

MARGARET: [*She is still holding him*] No you ain't.

JAMES: I'd like to feed you to some animal, get every last scrap
cleared away. [*He tries to get free*]

MARGARET: You ain't even apologized. You ain't even said
you're sorry.

JAMES: [*Pushes her so that she falls*] Get off.

[*At this moment, JOHN arrives*].

JOHN: Fucking hell. [*Grabs JAMES*] What you push my mother
for?

JAMES: I never pushed her.

JOHN: Bollocks.

JAMES: I was walking away. What's up with her, she don't seem
right in the head.

JOHN: So what you push her for?

JAMES: I'm sorry she fell over. All right? You ought to keep her
somewhere out of harm's way.

JOHN: I'll put you somewhere out of harm's way.

JAMES: Are you starting? Are you starting? Come on then, have a
taste. Have a try.

[*They are beginning to fight. REG, who has been working on a car
nearby, walks in, picks JAMES up and holds him midair*]

REG: Explain yourself.

JAMES: I never...

REG: Shut up.

JAMES: Calm down Reg.

REG: Do you want me to deck you?

JAMES: No I don't.

MARGARET: There was no call for that, was there. There was no call for what he done to me.

REG: None at all. I seen it.

JAMES: Something come over me. I thought she was my mum.

REG: Eh?

JAMES: Let me go, fuck you. I thought I was seeing things. I thought she was my mum come back to get me.

REG: [*Letting go*] Tell me, James, why would you want to throw down your mum on a concrete path?

MARGARET: I'm not to be upset. Am I John.

JOHN: Go indoors mum, have a lie down.

MARGARET: I ought to take one of them pills.

JOHN: You go in, I'll be in in a minute.

MARGARET: I ought to telephone to the police.

REG: Don't worry love, we'll take care of it. Won't we John.

MARGARET: They'll never come about that window. We shall have to board that up.

JOHN: What window?

JAMES: I never broke no fucking window.

REG: [*To JAMES*] Where's your wallet? [*JAMES gives it to him*] It's thicker than a fucking dictionary.

JAMES: That ain't mine, I got to hand it on.

REG: Hand it on less a hundred. [*He takes money out and gives it to JOHN*]

JAMES: Don't do that, man, you're getting me in shit.

REG: Shut your face.

JAMES: You'll get my fucking legs broken.

REG: You ought to have thought of that sooner.

JAMES: I never smashed no fucking window. I give you my word.

REG: I'm losing patience with you. This is John, tell him you apologize.

JAMES: I'm sorry about your mum.

JOHN: Yeah.

REG: What you want to do, John, you want to take it further?

JOHN: No use crying over spilt milk, is there. We're all neighbours
here.

REG: You're a philosopher. James could learn from you.

JOHN: I ought to go and see how she is.

REG: Good night then John.

JOHN: Good night. Thank you. [*He goes in*]

JAMES: If I come up a hundred short I'm dead. Who do you think
it's for.

REG: I don't want to know.

JAMES: You're a good friend, Reg. My friend.

REG: I am your friend.

JAMES: You think all you got to do is call yourself my friend and
you can shit on me to your heart's content.

REG: What's a hundred these days.

JAMES: You think I'm working for people who can't count.

REG: Perish the thought, you're too choosy ain't you.

JAMES: Fuck you.

REG: Here's fifty. You'll have to raise the other half by your own
efforts. Sell one of your trainers.

JAMES: The man's a cunt.

REG: Eh?

JAMES: He didn't have to take it, did he.

REG: I give it him.

JAMES: It's too much anyhow. He could fix another couple of
windows with that. I could go and bust them for him now.

REG: You owe that man a debt of gratitude. You're fortunate his
disposition is so pleasant.

JAMES: I don't trust any cunt that's pleasant. I don't trust any cunt
that forgives me what I done to them. What must they be
feeling, they must be all twisted up inside.

REG: John is a man who prefers to let bygones be bygones.

JAMES: So you think I made no impression.

REG: You made an impression James. I don't think you have to
worry. I hope that poor woman's all right. I'm going down the
pub in a minute, come and help me pack up.

[*REG goes. JAMES remains behind for a moment*]

JAMES: When someone finds fault with me, it interrupts my inner
life. Therefore I become violently angry. Technically they might
be in the right, in which case I might not enjoy my revenge.
But if they're in the wrong, I definitely will. I had to get that

woman off me. Being old is catching, you don't want to let it
touch you. Each time it touches you, you lose a bit more
immunity, you lose another life. They'll have a grudge against
me now. The fact is, when you wrong someone, you ought to
get on and finish the job. It's a shame to leave damaged people
wandering round. They're dangerous and they're ugly. [*He
goes*]

Scene 6

Reg and Sheila's home the following Sunday afternoon.
*[STEPHI is lying face down on the floor and SHEILA has her foot
on STEPHI's back. JAMES and MICHAEL are drinking]*

STEPHI: [*To herself*] Sundays with Sheila. They think the sun
    shines out of her. She gives herself out like prizes, rationed
    though, she's never at a loss. Some women must be differently
    made. I ain't got the detachment. I ain't got no interest in men
    I can get the better of. She's got an interest in getting the better
    of men she ain't got no interest in.

SHEILA: Hands by your sides. Relax yourself. A structural engineer
    taught me this.

STEPHI: What you going to do? [*SHEILA starts to walk along her
    back*] Shit!

SHEILA: What's wrong with you?

STEPHI: You'll put my back out.

SHEILA: I'm putting it in, love. Any pain you feel, it means
    you've got something that isn't where it ought to be. When I'm
    finished you'll have it all in the right place.

STEPHI: Where's that, Australia?

JAMES: Sheila.

SHEILA: Yes?

JAMES: Michael's got a back problem.

MICHAEL: Fuck off.

SHEILA: Have you, love?

JAMES: He's too embarrassed to talk about it.

SHEILA: You don't need to talk, Michael, get down on the floor.

MICHAEL: Thanks very much, it's all right thank you.

SHEILA: Lie down love.

*[MICHAEL obeys. SHEILA abandons STEPHI and starts to walk on
MICHAEL's back]*

JAMES: [*To STEPHI*] She's finished with you, she's got an urgent case.

SHEILA: Goodness, Michael, what a lot of lumps you got.

JAMES: You ought to see the other side.

SHEILA: I can feel every knob in your spine. Relax, Michael, I'm massaging you with my toes. I'll make you sore if you're stiff. Pretend the floor is made of rubber.

MICHAEL: Oh.

SHEILA: What's the matter?

JAMES: He can't feel it. [*Rubs his foot violently on the base of MICHAEL'S spine*]

MICHAEL: Christ! Get off!

[*He grabs JAMES by the ankle, pulls him to the ground and they start to wrestle, dislodging SHEILA*]

JAMES: You're over-reacting Michael. You're acting on impulse...

[*REG enters with a dish of squid salad*]

REG: Calamari. Who's having some? Stephi my love, you want feeding up, you got nothing there a man can get his hands on.

STEPHI: What is it?

REG: Calamari. Squid.

STEPHI: I'm not eating that.

REG: Ask yourself this. Why do you fear foreign food? "I'm not eating that," she says, "I ain't letting anything past my lips that ain't English".

STEPHI: Disgusting animals they are, all them legs.

REG: What's wrong with their legs? White and tasty, washed by the sea. Look at that. The English, if there ain't a nursery rhyme about it, they won't eat it. The English don't want to be adults. [*He eats*]

[*Doorbell. SHEILA goes to answer it. REG offers the dish to MICHAEL, who dubiously eats a piece of squid*]

SHEILA: [*Letting JOHN in*] Come on in love, ain't that nice that you decided to come along. He brought me a six-pack. Ain't you a man of the world, not like this other rubbish. [*To the others*] I expect you know John.

REG: John will eat calamari. John is a man of vision.

JOHN: That's right. If I see it, I eat it.

JAMES: Why does he smell of air freshener? What did you put on yourself, John? Was it Airwick?

JOHN: Disinfectant. In case I met you.

JAMES: It don't smell like disinfectant. It smells overpoweringly sweet, like the stuff in the little plastic holder that people leave on the back of the toilet to disguise the smell of shit.

REG: Come and sit down, John. Ignore the banter.

JAMES: Reg wants to hug you, cos he's a hugging man.

REG: Are you going to keep a civil tongue in your head? Or am I going to push you through the wall?

JAMES: You're masterful Reg. You're a godsend to us young ones. Ain't you got any friends your own age?

REG: You can piss off out of here.

JAMES: Yeah. You can patronize someone else. I see right through you. Stephi?

STEPHI: Off you go then.

JAMES: Suit yourself. Michael?

SHEILA: Michael's going to stay and tell me all about his back.

JAMES: Michael?

MICHAEL: Catch you later, man.

JAMES: Fuck you too. [*He goes*]

REG: If he'd have been my son, he wouldn't have lived to grow up and embarrass me.

JOHN: I ought to have picked a different time.

REG: How can anyone excuse behaviour like that? That's the problem I'm facing. Eh Stephi?

STEPHI: I'm sorry he was so rude. I don't know what possessed him.

JOHN: Didn't he tell you we'd met before?

REG: The less said about that the better.

SHEILA: Me and Reg don't like nastiness. We're too old for it. The thing with James is to give him space. Let him rave. I would never oppose him directly, no. Little by little I would seem to agree with him while gradually bringing in a different point of view. The object is, to lead him on to think that he might have been being just that little bit hotheaded. He'll never admit to it mind. He's a little terror. He oughtn't to be let loose.

REG: James needs a rock. I would never cut myself off. Because he needs to understand that a man has got a soul, and a soul is a thing that never changes. You turn to it and it's always there. Physical strength is a pale image of the strength in a soul. He thinks we're soft.

SHEILA: Not me, he don't.

REG: He thinks we're fucking soft. I'm not enamoured of going round frightening people. I don't enjoy it. I've been bodyguard, rent collector and avenger. I've hurt people physically. I know how to set fires so it looks as if they sprang up by magic. I can make a fuse box sing. Most of life's problems are very simple. If someone causes you offence, adjust their piping with a monkey wrench. Or block their sewer with a brick. Calamari, John?

JOHN: Oh. Thank you.

REG: Michael?

MICHAEL: Got to go to the bog. [*He goes*]

STEPHI: Ain't you got anything civilized to eat? Packet of crisps?

REG: God in heaven, Stephanie, I'll find you a biscuit. [*He goes to the kitchen*]

SHEILA: He don't know where they are. [*She follows him*]

JOHN: I ain't seen you.

STEPHI: I'm out cleaning most days.

JOHN: Where's that?

STEPHI: Round Elgin Road. James don't like it. That's why I do it.

JOHN: What else will you do that James don't like?

STEPHI: That's a funny question.

JOHN: Women in your situation will generally look to their own best interests.

STEPHI: What's wrong with my situation?

JOHN: Your situation is shit.

STEPHI: You got a right to your opinion.

JOHN: No, I didn't mean that. What I meant was...

[*SHEILA comes in with a packet of biscuits. REG and MICHAEL also appear*]

SHEILA: [*Throwing the biscuits to STEPHI*] Catch, love.

REG: Arm wrestle, John. Over here.

JOHN: Not on your life.

SHEILA: Did you see on the telly last night about American women's false tits? The surgeon has to use his full strength to get one of them in. Who would have thought a woman's chest could put up so much resistance? Come and sit down, Michael, tell us your views.

MICHAEL: They ought to invent something natural. [*He sits*]

Scene 7

John's house.

[JOHN comes through his front door into his sitting room, which contains items of furniture that he has been working on]

JOHN: Fool! Amateur! Turd! I made a complete fucking fool of myself. She was well impressed. She wouldn't have minded at all if I'd seeped out through the floor. "You got a right to your opinion". Bitch! On the other hand. On the other hand. What was that about "James don't like it". There's a message there. I ought to think about that. She's telling me something there. She ain't aware of it, that's all. Next time I see her, I'll be ready. Next time I see her, she'd better watch out. Oh fuck. I made a total bollocks of it. Kami-fucking-kaze. *[Starts to work, sanding wood]* Her James didn't stay long. He can't forgive me for his own fucking bad behaviour. There must be another side to him. The cunt must be lovable in some way. Otherwise they all love him for being a cunt, don't they. Which is absurd. It's unfortunate that I upset him, though. He's right next door. I feel like I'm a mouse with a cat outside. No matter how big a mouse is, it sees things from the mouse's point of view. What does the superior man do in such a case? Blot out the negative, be twice as positive. The fact is, he's a potential friend. We got mutual dislike in common.

MARGARET: *[Entering]* You're back are you?

JOHN: Yes.

MARGARET: I didn't know you was back.

JOHN: No.

MARGARET: Are you doing that sanding now?

JOHN: That's right.

MARGARET: Nasty dust it makes.

JOHN: I'll clean it up later.

MARGARET: Sawdust over everything. Look at the couch beside you. That will get down into the fabric. You'll never get rid of that. That will eat its way down.

JOHN: I'll hoover it up when I'm finished.

MARGARET: I can hardly move in here for your mess. I can hardly turn round. You ought not to take up so much space.

JOHN: Got to be active, haven't I.

MARGARET: When you was a boy you used to keep to your room.

JOHN: Yes, quite right, you kept me contained.

MARGARET: When you was a baby you was tiny.

JOHN: I got to make a living.

MARGARET: You ought to have more consideration.

JOHN: I can't leave you, see.

MARGARET: That's what you say. You say I can't manage.

JOHN: You're all right.

MARGARET: I can't, can I.

JOHN: You manage.

MARGARET: I ain't been eating right. I ain't been looked after.

JOHN: I look after you. You're all right. You was always a bit
      forgetful. Nobody's fault, is it.

MARGARET: Raising you brought me to this.

JOHN: And me. Nothing wrong with it, is there. I look after you,
      don't I.

MARGARET: I want the telly switched on.

JOHN: Switch it on then.

MARGARET: I can't hear it with your racket.

JOHN: Switch it on, I'll be finished in a minute.

MARGARET: Never mind.

[*MARGARET sits in silence while JOHN continues to work*]

JOHN: [*Stops*] Fuck this.

MARGARET: You watch your mouth.

JOHN: I don't mean to make you unhappy.

MARGARET: You can't help it, can you.

JOHN: No.

MARGARET: You going to switch it on then?

[*JOHN switches on the television*]

Scene 8

Next day.

[*MICHAEL carries a bag of newspapers, and is putting some
through James' door. JAMES comes out*]

JAMES: I thought it was you.

MICHAEL: Paper.

JAMES: Call that a paper.

MICHAEL: I'll be off then.

JAMES: [*Extracting papers from the door*] South East Gazette. Five
      copies. [*Drops four on the ground*] That bag's getting lighter by
      the minute. Why don't you deliver us some more [*Takes a*

handful of papers out of Michael's bag, drops them] No point
pushing them through all them letterboxes, it only shreds them.

MICHAEL: I thought you wouldn't be pleased to see me.

JAMES: But you brought me a paper. What you do that for? What
are your stars?

MICHAEL: Virgo.

JAMES: [*Looking for the astrology column*] Virgos are critical.
They fasten on others' weaknesses. Here you go. "Professional
colleagues will want to bounce ideas off you, and you'll have
plenty to say in return." You are definitely a Virgo, are you?

MICHAEL: Eh?

JAMES: "Spend Wednesday with the love of your life." Who's the
love of your life, Michael?

MICHAEL: Marilyn Monroe.

JAMES: It says here, spend Wednesday with her "and there will be
some exciting surprises". Like finding out she's got bits of
blue-tack stuck to the back of her. "Call me if you want to
know more. Julian Trent." Fucked if I will, you squeezy-faced
little chiseller. [*He drops the paper on the ground*]

MICHAEL: Better get on.

JAMES: If you want.

MICHAEL: You ain't offended then.

JAMES: Who's offended. If anyone's offended, it's you.

MICHAEL: That's all right.

JAMES: Thank you. What did I do?

MICHAEL: Nothing.

JAMES: If I done nothing, why do you say, "that's all right"? I done
something, right? What did I do?

MICHAEL: I never said you done anything.

JAMES: Yes you did.

MICHAEL: I never said nothing.

JAMES: Like you never said nothing yesterday. You let me walk
out of there on my own.

MICHAEL: We all got a choice.

JAMES: You made your choice, didn't you.

MICHAEL: Reg is my friend.

JAMES: Reg ought to know better.

MICHAEL: Leave Reg out of it. Reg is like a father to you. Reg
can't do enough for you. He's a great man. He's a teacher.
Everything I've learned is down to Reg.

JAMES: Well that's a feather in his cap.

MICHAEL: Yeah, it is.

JAMES: So you're loyal to Reg then.

MICHAEL: A man without loyalty is no better than a devil.

JAMES: It's a shame you ain't loyal to me.

MICHAEL: I ought to smash you for that.

JAMES: No point crying about it. Maybe we're changing, going our separate ways.

MICHAEL: Don't talk to me like a stranger. It's a liberty. We're close, man.

JAMES: What's close?

MICHAEL: We got energy between us. I would never deny energy. I would never turn my back on my friend. I'd defend you the same as if I was defending myself.

JAMES: I can manage, thanks all the same.

MICHAEL: Just don't accuse me, all right?

JAMES: What you think of John then. All have a good time did you?

MICHAEL: He's all right.

JAMES: Did you see the way he looks for a little joke. Like he sees it scurrying past, a little joke running across the floor. He's got to catch it and pop it in the conversation. You see his eyes get wild and nervous. Will he get it. Should he make a lunge for it. Rate him, do you?

MICHAEL: I hadn't thought about it.

JAMES: I wonder if he's still looking for them little jokes when he's at home. Searching desperately, alone with his mum. "John, John, I've trod in something. Get it off my shoe." "Certainly. Christ, it's a little joke. You've squashed it. Never mind, can't afford to waste it, I'll clean it off and it will do for Michael." I forgot. You never met her. You're the friend that chucked a fucking brick through the fucking window and left me to take your fucking heat.

MICHAEL: You're too fucking slow.

JAMES: Slow. She come out the door like she was on a fucking spring. Like a fucking cuckoo clock.She was hanging on to my clothes, I couldn't get rid of her...

[MARGARET emerges from her house pushing or carrying a piece of John's furniture. She is talking to herself. She leaves it outside and goes in to fetch some more]

JAMES: Well. That's exhibit A.

MICHAEL: She's inspired.

JAMES: John strips down furniture, don't he. That's because he wants to better himself. He don't want to remain among the understains.

[*MARGARET comes out with another piece of furniture*]

MICHAEL: She don't know we're here.

MARGARET: [*To JAMES and MICHAEL*] I can't be doing with it indoors. I ain't got room to swing a cat. He's got a grandfather in there.

JAMES: You'll be telling me he's got a father next.

MARGARET: It's too heavy. I can't shift it. Will you shift it for me?

JAMES: Shift what, darling?

MARGARET: Shift it out here.

JAMES: Oh I'll shift it. Any place you like.

MARGARET: I want it all out here and out from under my feet.

JAMES: Course you do.

MARGARET: Come on then.

JAMES: What's your son going to say?

MARGARET: He's got no right. He's taking up too much space.

JAMES: Yeah. He is.

MARGARET: [*Leading them into the house*] He's making me tired half to death.

[*JAMES and MICHAEL emerge carrying a grandfather clock, which they put with the other items. MARGARET speaks through the door just before she closes it*]

MARGARET: Much obliged.

JAMES: That's all right. [*Sotto voce*] Now go and have a look for your mind, when's the last time you had it?

MARGARET: Good boys, good boys. [*She shuts the door*]

MICHAEL: Stuff won't last five minutes out here.

JAMES: You're right.

[*JAMES picks up a newspaper from the ground, crumples it, starts to stack paper round the furniture*]

MICHAEL: What you doing?

JAMES: You give me an idea all of a sudden.

MICHAEL: Wait up.

JAMES: Don't want it nicked, do we.

MICHAEL: This is a bad idea. It's mindless.

JAMES: Yeah, I thought you'd like it. Come on, it's as dry as tinder. It'll go up lovely. Magic.

MICHAEL: It's worth hundreds, man.

JAMES: You want to nick it, don't you.

MICHAEL: Yeah.

JAMES: Don't be so bourgeois.

MICHAEL: Antiques, ain't it.

JAMES: For yuppies. That clock looks embarrassed. It never expected to find itself here. People ought to tread that wormy depressing old crud underfoot, get some self-respect. [*Takes out his cigarette lighter*] Come on, we ain't got all day.

[*MICHAEL collects papers to add to the pile. JAMES lights his cigarette lighter*]

☐

ACT TWO

Scene 1

Tuesday morning in the flat of JAMES, STEPHI and LIZ.
[LIZ is eating breakfast. JAMES comes in from a bedroom]

JAMES: Fucking quiet, you are. I been lying in bed hearing you being fucking quiet. That fucking drawer. You been sliding it in and out like you was putting it under a fucking microscope. How many times do you have to open the fucking thing to get a fucking spoon. And when you got it, what the fuck do you do with it. Why do you have to stroke it round the bottom of your fucking cup without moving the fucking coffee. Can't you fucking stir it.

LIZ: You got sleep in the corners of your eyes.

JAMES: This place stinks.

LIZ: Don't you want a tissue?

JAMES: Your vermin are stinking us out.

LIZ: I give them a dusting down with talcum powder yesterday. Go and smell them if you like, it's mimosa. *[Silence]* I found two of your fag ends in the nest with them.

JAMES: Naughty little mice.

LIZ: They don't know tobacco's poison, do they.

JAMES: If it's poison, why don't the bastards die. They're the master race. They'll be here a million years from now, when all of us are fucking fossil fuel.

LIZ: Someone was asking for you last night.

JAMES: Yes.

LIZ: He seemed very upset.

JAMES: Yes.

LIZ: He said he was intending to call the police. He said his mind was made up.

JAMES: Whose mind was this.

LIZ: I hope you won't be annoyed.

JAMES: Bollocks. You hope I will be annoyed, and I am fucking annoyed, so you've got what you wanted, ain't you.

LIZ: Did you help the woman next door carry out some furniture yesterday?

JAMES: He's talking to the pigs, is he.

LIZ: Only someone set light to it.

JAMES: What a shame.

LIZ: I wonder what made you the way you are. I used to pray to God to take you away and bring me a little sister.

JAMES: Straight to the pigs. The man's a zero.

LIZ: Your games was never constructive.

JAMES: What's your opinion then. You assume I put a fucking match to it.

LIZ: If they put you in prison, mind you don't do away with yourself in your cell. A lot of young men have wound up in the papers on account of that.

JAMES: What proof has he got. He's got no more proof than you. You'll never know the truth and you don't want to know the truth. You know what you want to know.

LIZ: They get so desperate, there was one that dug the veins out of his wrist with his dinner fork. They only give them spoons now.

JAMES: You hate me.

LIZ: But it's too easy, ain't it. I mean to say, if them officers don't like you for any reason. Three against one, what chance would somebody have. They're all trained in self defence.

JAMES: So if the pigs was to come asking after me, what would you say.

LIZ: They've got no reason to ask me.

JAMES: Wanting to know my alibi.

LIZ: I'd say I didn't know.

JAMES: Would you.

LIZ: What else would I say.

JAMES: If I was to get nicked, there are people who'd be worried. Know what I mean.

LIZ: No.

JAMES: People I work with sometimes. You wouldn't take to them. They might think I was telling tales, see.

LIZ: You ain't got no tales to tell. You're only their errand boy.

JAMES: You know a lot about it.

LIZ: That's what Reg says.

JAMES: What Reg says don't interest me. Reg is a geriatric sniffing round the hole where his life used to be. If they was to think I was telling tales, you might find them calling. They might take it out on you, see, thinking it would upset me.

LIZ: They wouldn't think it would upset you if they knew you.

JAMES: All I'm saying is, be loyal. Be my sister. Then you got no
worries. If the pigs ask you, tell them I was here. That sorts it.

LIZ: You want me to tell a lie for you.

JAMES: Please.

LIZ: I'll think about it. What will you give me.

JAMES: How much do you want.

LIZ: Oh I don't want money. No.

JAMES: What you want.

LIZ: You think of something. I can't think.

JAMES: Oh for fuck's sake. Do you want a dress?

LIZ: I don't think so. You're always trying to dress me up, ain't
you, making out you're ashamed of me.

JAMES: Do you want a watch?

LIZ: I got a watch. I don't need two watches, do I.

JAMES: How does anyone know what you need.

LIZ: I don't have needs. You're the one that has needs.

[STEPHI and SHEILA arrive]

SHEILA: Frowsting here, look at you James. Why don't you come
to the pool with us next Tuesday. It uses a whole different set
of muscles, don't it Steph.

STEPHI: I couldn't walk up the bleeding steps, my legs was going
from under me.

SHEILA: He's lovely though, ain't he. I'd like to clone him. I want
one just like him to take home with me. How are you Liz, all
right.

LIZ: Yes thank you.

JAMES: It's too early for me. I'm off back to bed.

SHEILA: Ain't you going to have a coffee.

JAMES: No, it would only keep me awake.

[He goes]

SHEILA: [To LIZ] What about you. Why don't you come swimming
one of these days.

LIZ: I wouldn't like that. I wouldn't like to make a spectacle of
myself.

SHEILA: Not much chance of that is there?

LIZ: You never know what's in that water, do you.

STEPHI: Yeah, you might get pregnant, Liz.

SHEILA: No she wouldn't, they sterilize it, don't they.

LIZ: I'd never be able to put my face in.

SHEILA: Some people say it's boring. It is. It's very, very boring. But that's the challenge, ain't it, to find the excitement within the boredom. Some days I wake up and I really don't want to go. But I persuade myself, because I can always get the better of myself, I've had that much practice on other people. You get down there and you get in the water and start trogging up and down, and your body don't want to join in, it's like hauling yourself through wet concrete, which of course some people might enjoy. Anyway, you keep going and after a while you loosen up, and then you begin to feel the benefit. Because there's something about being in the water, scientists have proved that it releases the ecstasy in your brain. All you got to do is keep on with them rhythmic movements and chemicals are created that uplift you, take away your pain, and put you in touch with your inner source of happiness. It's so easy to lose that.

STEPHI: There was this man kept brushing up against me.

SHEILA: I got a frog kick like a mule.

STEPHI: Guess who give me a letter yesterday. He come up to me at the bus stop. John. He says to me, "how do you spell your name". So I told him and he says, "Then this must be for you", gives me this letter he's written and walks off. He's off his trolley.

LIZ: What did it say.

STEPHI: It said, "Dear Stephanie. You know the rest. John".

SHEILA: Not much of a letter. He wants you to write it for him, does he.

STEPHI: He was making up to me at your house.

SHEILA: On Sunday. He never had the chance.

STEPHI: You saw to that.

LIZ: It's time I was off.

SHEILA: You'd think he'd have more sense.

LIZ: If you give them the wrong impression and they think they can do what they like, then you've only got yourself to blame I always think. Not that I'm an expert. I'll be back this evening. [She goes]

SHEILA: Someone's got grit in their spinach.

STEPHI: She drives me mental. She picks at you like a little child picking at its plate. In the kitchen she's disgusting, she slops around with a wet cloth and leaves it lying anywhere. Wherever she's been, there's tissues dropped like tears from the heavens. She stuffs them down the furniture. She stuffs them in her clothes and they spring out at you. She's always trying to tell me what James likes. James don't like his toast that dark. James won't use a 60-watt light bulb. James gets pains in his feet. I could tell her what brings them on. He won't move out of here, see, he reckons she ought to move, he don't want to lose this place. But she can't move, can she. All her tissues are here. Stuffed into the cracks.

SHEILA: Yes, she's put down roots, bless her.

STEPHI: It's a wonder James ain't worse.

SHEILA: He come round yesterday, did he tell you that? He apologized on account of what happened Sunday. So I says to him, it's Reg you ought to be apologizing to, and he says, "Fuck that, I know what side my bread's buttered". He does too. Reg don't understand that he and James aren't the same age. James is older, the little devil. He plays Reg along, I can see him doing it, and he bleeding well knows I can.

STEPHI: You don't want to indulge him on my account.

SHEILA: I don't indulge him. That's just what I don't do. You got to let them know where they stand. The way he speaks to you, if he was to try that with me, by the time I finished with him, he wouldn't know if he was Arthur or fucking Martha.

STEPHI: Is that what you done to Reg.

SHEILA: Reg looks after me and I look after him.

STEPHI: Problems. Who needs them. But if we hadn't got them we wouldn't know we was alive, would we.

SHEILA: I don't care to be too knowing.

STEPHI: Most people have got a memory that connects everything up. That's where James is superior. He don't make the connections. He's got no way of knowing what anyone means to him. He's supernatural.

SHEILA: Is he?

STEPHI: He can promise you anything, because he don't keep his promises. He floats.

SHEILA: Does he.

STEPHI: He's moody. He can't lie still at night. He grinds his teeth. Nobody unnatural can really be happy, can they. They might be ahead of the game but they won't be happy, will they.

SHEILA: No.

STEPHI: I want to make him happy. Then he'll know what the rest of us have got to go through.

SHEILA: Yes, good for you love.

[*The doorbell. STEPHI goes. Comes back in*]

STEPHI: James! It's the police to see you.

Scene 2

Tuesday evening. A pub.

[*MICHAEL is sitting at a table with LIZ. Telephone some distance away*]

LIZ: It's ever so nice of Reg.

MICHAEL: Yeah.

LIZ: You find out who your friends are.

MICHAEL: Yeah. Soon be here.

LIZ: Do you think so? Only I ought to get back soon, I'll be missing my programme. It's only on of a Tuesday. Although I missed it last week. The reason was, I lost my hairbrush. There's nothing more frustrating, is there.

MICHAEL: No.

LIZ: Not that I needed it, but you know how it is, once a thing goes missing you can't rest until you find it, can you. It's the thin end of the wedge. I turned the house upside down. I couldn't remember the last time I'd used it, my mind was an absolute blank. Panic will do that, won't it.

MICHAEL: Yeah, definitely.

LIZ: The worst of it is, I began to get this itching in my scalp, until soon I was ready to pull out all my hairs one by one. That wouldn't have solved anything, would it.

MICHAEL: You wouldn't need a hairbrush then.

LIZ: Do you know what I did?

MICHAEL: No.

LIZ: I prayed. I said to God, "is there something I'm doing wrong? Tell me what it is". Just then I thought I'd wash out my yellow jersey which I'd been intending to do, but putting it off, you know, I'm inclined to put things off, and I picked it up, and guess what fell out. Do you believe in the supernatural?

MICHAEL: Some of it.

LIZ: I hope everything's gone smoothly down the nick, don't you.

MICHAEL: Bound to.

LIZ: Yes I expect you're right. How's your mum keeping?

MICHAEL: She's in Rio.

LIZ: Oh lovely. Been to see her, have you.

MICHAEL: Yeah.

LIZ: It must be lovely there, is it? Subtropical. I imagine the life is very different there.

MICHAEL: Yeah. She give me some sun glasses.

LIZ: That's my drink finished.

MICHAEL: You want another.

LIZ: Just a single if you don't mind.

[*MICHAEL gets up, goes to the phone, waves to LIZ to show that he'll be getting the drinks in a moment. He dials. Listens. Breathes heavily. Hangs up. Waits. Dials again*]

MICHAEL: [*In a disguised voice, not heard by LIZ*] Where you been all this time. I been trying urgently to reach you... A friend. Listen. I got some advice for you. You didn't ought to leave your mother on her own. She's liable to get frightened out of her wits. You don't want that, do you... Don't threaten me. I got a message to tell you... No it ain't James. It's a friend of James. James has got a lot of friends. How could it be James. No-one knows better than you where James is. You put him there. The pigs come for him this morning, didn't they. You'll be seeing him soon enough. They won't detain him long. Ain't you feeling well. You didn't ought to be. If I was you I'd be shitting myself. This is the message. It's from James. He says to tell you he once knew a guy that grassed. Are you listening. This is important. He wants you to know what they done to this guy. They took him for a ride in the country and hammered a six-inch nail in his neck, but unfortunately he made so much noise they had to split his head open with a shovel, and they said when his brains come out they smelled disgusting, a real traitor smell...

[*JOHN has hung up. MICHAEL puts down the phone and goes off to get the drinks as REG, STEPHI, SHEILA and JAMES arrive and join LIZ*]

REG: End of a perfect day. James is buying.

STEPHI: I will. What you having Sheil?

SHEILA: My name is Sheila, my weakness is tequila.

JAMES: [*To STEPHI*] Sit down.

LIZ: Michael's looking after me, thanks all the same.

[*JAMES goes off to buy drinks*]

REG: [*To LIZ*] They never even booked him. He was coming out
    the door by the time we got down there. I had the bail money
    in my hand.

LIZ: Fancy them taking him down there if they wasn't intending to
    book him. You'd think they'd have more idea, wouldn't you.

STEPHI: Would you have rather they locked him up?

REG: Don't be sensitive girl, she never meant it like that, did you
    Liz. We're here to celebrate. Ours not to reason why.

STEPHI: What you say?

REG: Never mind what I said.

STEPHI: Well, he's free, ain't he.

REG: Free as air.

LIZ: There's nothing they can do, is there.

SHEILA: James is a lucky boy.

REG: I can't think why that John didn't come to me.

SHEILA: Out of order, going public like that. James will resent that.
    That will lead to trouble, that will.

STEPHI: He might have resented getting his stuff torched.

SHEILA: That's not the point, is it. We all get problems.

REG: But we don't go giving out names.

STEPHI: I would.

REG: I put up with a lot from you Stephanie. You talk a lot of
    cobblers. But you're James's friend so we keep our mouths
    shut. If only you could pay us the same compliment. You're a
    nice-looking girl except you talk shit. You understand fuck-all
    about how mankind lives. You girls, you're living in a different
    world. You sit up in the stands waving a handkerchief, you
    don't want to know what it's like on the field. Why does a man
    fuck a woman? I'll tell you. Because he wants her to know
    what he knows. He wants to pass it on. But a girl like you just
    don't get the message. You got a hard heart, Stephanie. All you
    want to do is sit in judgment.

SHEILA: I expect it was only intended as a bit of fun.

REG: Once the pigs get hold of you, you never know what people
    are going to think you told them. Plus, you never know what
    you're going to tell them.

SHEILA: James knows what to tell them.

REG: Fucking right. Every fucking thing he ever fucking knew, and

if anyone was to say, that ain't fucking much, he'd say, wait
up, I got more, and he'd compose the entire thousand fucking
nights for them cunts, not forgetting the one extra fucker.

SHEILA: Fine friend you are.

REG: We do our friends no favours by muddled thinking.

SHEILA: Some of us know how to think without moving our lips.

REG: Some of us wouldn't move our lips if our arse was on fire.

STEPHI: James ain't weak.

REG: He's weak as piss. He's so weak it's a form of strength.

SHEILA: [To REG] You're saying, everything you stand for, James
don't give a toss for it.

REG: That's right.

SHEILA: He don't give a toss for you.

REG: Nor you.

SHEILA: But you can't keep your distance.

REG: My distance. Bleeding Christ on high. Ask yourself this. What
is my distance? Who's to say what my distance is? Anyone
telling me what my distance is better be fucking sure what their
own distance is, because it seems to me their distance is not so
much fact as fantasy. And fantasy is all some people have got.
Where's my beer?

LIZ: That John has only stored up trouble for himself. I hope he
knows what he done.

[JAMES and MICHAEL come back with the drinks]

JAMES: Who?

SHEILA: It's a shame they didn't charge you love, I been planning
your campaign. "Free James. He was only arson about".

JAMES: Who was you talking about? Judas?

STEPHI: You don't even know it was him. It could have been his
mum that said.

JAMES: Oh definitely. Keep an open mind. It's important to you.

STEPHI: I will.

JAMES: Think the best of him. Why not. Think the worst of me.
You do, don't you. Tell the world what a cunt I am. Be
perfectly honest.

STEPHI: I am.

JAMES: That's right. Blacken my name.

REG: No-one's blackening anybody's name. We love you, James.
We come here to share with you. You don't want to be
downhearted. You got friends looking out for you. Ain't he,

Michael.

MICHAEL: Yeah.

REG: And you and your friends are going to get rat-arsed, because that's what friends are for. Alcohol is a solvent. It solves. It goes through your system like petrol, cutting out the tarnish and leaving it as shiny, bright and clean as the day you were born. Soon you'll be lit up inside like a colourful juke box, and music will come out. Won't it Michael.

MICHAEL: [*To James*] To vengeance eh?

SHEILA: [*A toast*] To liberty.

[*They drink. JOHN appears at the door of the pub. Stares at them. JAMES speaks, aside*]

JAMES: He seems upset. The way they're staring at him I'm not surprised. I don't think he'll come back in this pub for a while. Even he must be getting the feeling he's about to trip over someone's feet with his head. Such a lot to learn, where's he supposed to begin. They don't want you, John. You got bad presentation. They look at you, they see a man that's easily damaged. That's the last thing they want to be reminded of, that people are easily damaged. Because they're people. I ain't a person. I'm less than a person and more than a person. I'm a cutting edge. Because metal is not so easily damaged. Never mind who told me that. What I get told in here [*Strokes his temple*] is nobody's business but mine and them that tells me. [*JOHN leaves*]

SHEILA: Ain't it embarrassing. He ought to know better than to come in here.

MICHAEL: Insensitive cunt.

JAMES: He just realized, he came without his little joke. He'll have to go back for it.

Scene 3

Outside John and Margaret's door. A fortnight later. Graffiti. Their dustbin has been emptied on the doorstep.

[*JOHN comes out, speaking to MARGARET who is somewhere behind him*]

JOHN: Come on. I got your cardigan. [*Sees the mess on the doorstep. Hastily clears it up*] They got them little bakewells in that shop.

MARGARET: [*From inside*] They make them too sweet. They
    didn't ought to make them as sweet as that. [*She appears*] Have
    I got my purse?

JOHN: You got it in your bag.

MARGARET: [*Starts going through her bag*] Hold these.

JOHN: What you want all these safety pins for.

MARGARET: Hold on to my hand lotion. I ain't got any lipstick
    on. [*She is taking her lipstick out of her bag*]

JOHN: Yes you have.

MARGARET: Have I got it on? Where's my mirror? [*Finds a
    mirror, looks in it*] Fancy that. I put my lipstick on and forgot
    my tooth.

JOHN: You don't need your tooth. Who you going to bite? It's
    broad daylight.

MARGARET: There's the phone. Ain't you going to answer it?

JOHN: No.

MARGARET: What, is it them again? You ought to get the police
    on them. You ought not to let it go on.

JOHN: I don't know who it is, do I.

MARGARET: Them phone calls have been going on and on.

JOHN: Twelve days and twelve nights.

MARGARET: Did I find my purse?

JOHN: Yes.

MARGARET: No I never. You're imagining things.

JOHN: Come on. I ain't going to wait all day.

MARGARET: Don't rush me. I get confused if I'm rushed.

JOHN: We'll get some of them bakewells, won't we.

MARGARET: You can if you want. They're too sweet for me.
    Who's going to look after the house?

JOHN: Can't stay here all the time, can we. We can't stay in that
    house for the rest of our lives.

MARGARET: Someone ought to look after it. You go on down the
    shop. Buy yourself something nice. Wait a minute and I'll get
    you a pound. [*Rummages*]

JOHN: I don't want a pound mum. I want you to come down the
    shop with me. You need a change of scene. If you ain't
    coming, I ain't going.

MARGARET: Who's going to get the shopping then?

JOHN: No-one.

MARGARET: Don't you defy me.

JOHN: You'll have to do without. Are you coming?

MARGARET: I'll go hungry, thank you.

JOHN: You will.

MARGARET: I know I will. Nobody cares, do they.

JOHN: You ain't been out the door for the last ten days. Have you. You're afraid to come out the door.

MARGARET: I been out.

JOHN: Where?

MARGARET: To the shop.

JOHN: What did you buy?

MARGARET: All the necessities.

JOHN: Where are they?

MARGARET: Get more if you ain't satisfied.

JOHN: If you been out, you can come out now, can't you.

MARGARET: I can come out when I want.

JOHN: Show me. Come out here.

MARGARET: What for.

JOHN: Show me if you can.

MARGARET: I ain't a performing seal.

JOHN: What you want from the shop?

MARGARET: I don't know. You better get some of them little bakewells.

JOHN: Nice and sweet, are they.

MARGARET: Too sweet.

JOHN: How many shall I get?

MARGARET: Get us a couple of packets while you're there.

JOHN: One thing.

MARGARET: Yes? What you want?

JOHN: Step out here before I go. Show me you can step out here. Then I'll go down the shop for you.

MARGARET: What's the point of that? There's no point to it.

JOHN: Do it to please me.

MARGARET: What you going to do?

JOHN: Nothing.

MARGARET: I don't do things for no reason.

JOHN: Show me you ain't afraid to come out.

MARGARET: I've got nothing to be afraid of. I done nothing to be ashamed of. It's you that's brought all this trouble on our heads. They told me that on the phone. [*She goes in, slamming the door*]

JOHN: She forgets everything except who to blame. Nobody's life is perfect. I can't do more. I can't even make her smile. I can't even flirt with her, bullshit her, raise her spirits. I'd have to raise my own. Despair is the ultimate sin. The superior man will fend it off. I'll get her them little cakes. They pissed through the letterbox last night. I wish I'd heard them. Madame Guillotine. Then I'd burn the door. Burn everything they've touched. Burn the house. Basically it ain't the house's fault. Burn myself. I don't want to catch them. I don't want to know who they are, or how many they are. What's the difference. People are all much the same. So long as I don't see them, no permanent harm is done. In days to come, when all this is forgotten, I might get to know them. It will be forgotten. I'm capable of forgetting it now. My mind can slip away to where I'm sitting in the pub with them. Reg is there, telling us how to manufacture explosives, and Sheila's getting too close, and Stephi's there looking nice. It'll never happen. I feel like they've seen my insides. I feel like some disgusting freak of nature.

[*STEPHI arrives carrying bags of shopping, on the way to her door*]

JOHN: Are you going to walk right past?

STEPHI: I didn't see you there.

JOHN: I didn't know I blended in so well.

STEPHI: I got to go.

JOHN: You seem embarrassed.

STEPHI: I got my reasons ain't I?

JOHN: I been wishing I could talk to you.

STEPHI: I'm sorry about what's happened.

JOHN: I been getting phone calls in the middle of the night. You know what I mean? Two skips I never ordered come to my door last week.

STEPHI: I'm sorry.

JOHN: And fourteen speciality pizzas.

STEPHI: I don't hold with it.

JOHN: I've had some very unusual post.

STEPHI: People don't know when to stop.

JOHN: Nobody speaks to me. Strangers look away from me. Everybody knows just one thing about me, which is that I'm to be avoided. You're part of it. I still can't believe it.

STEPHI: Not really.

JOHN: One look from you and I'd be revived. I'd wake up out of this as if I was in heaven. How can you refuse to give me something I need so much? You aren't what you seem. You're some kind of cold-hearted puppet made to deceive me. You're so lifelike and tender-looking, you must have been made by the devil himself. Don't go.

STEPHI: I got to get inside with these bags.

JOHN: Put them down. Give them to me.

STEPHI: I got to go. There's nothing I can do.

JOHN: You been shopping for his food. It's heavy. I'll take it to the door for you.

STEPHI: I can manage.

JOHN: I ain't jealous. You want to feed him, I'll help you. I'd spoon it in his mouth if it meant I could be near you.

[REG and JAMES emerge through STEPHI's front door]

STEPHI: Hullo Reg.

REG: Hullo Steph.

JAMES: You planning to come in? [STEPHI goes in through the door, watched by the others] I'll be back in a minute, all right? [Shuts the door. Meanwhile JOHN has been trying to unlock his front door] Trying to get it in are you? What's your problem?

JOHN: Go and fuck yourself.

JAMES: Mind your fingers. [JOHN gets through his door and shuts it] What's he doing talking to her. What's he playing at. I ain't going to stand for that.

REG: Then you'll have to call him out. Explain your feelings. Half a broken bottle in the face can generally be relied upon to put Cupid to flight.

JAMES: I can't understand her.

REG: A plank with a couple of nails sticking out can often be found lying conveniently to hand. In no way is the man who picks up such a plank in the heat of the moment guilty of intent.

JAMES: She knows my feelings. She done wrong to let him speak to her.

REG: A heavy spanner, or a hammer normally used for bashing out the rims of tyres, can easily enter into a combat of this sort when feelings are running high and normal restraint and good manners have been cast aside. The simplest weapon is often the most effective.

JAMES: Oh shut it you goon.

REG: It's better than ringing on the fucking doorbell and hiding
    round the corner. That's your level.
JAMES: You want to see my head bashed in?
REG: Can't stand here dreaming all day. Are you coming to help
    me sort this motor?
JAMES: Might as well.
[*They leave*]

Scene 4

Evening of the same day.
[*STEPHI is sitting in the yard of her house, at the back*]
STEPHI: So I spoke with who I shouldn't. I got a mind of my own,
    haven't I. The black looks I got. He looked ready to throw me
    across the street. He looked ready to break my ribs. Why don't
    he come back. Not late, though, is it. It ain't late enough to
    start feeling like I will do later. I'm enjoying the sunset. No
    point suffering in advance, is there. James. It ain't jealousy.
    Any excuse to punish me. If someone was begging at his feet
    he'd punish them twice over for embarrassing him. If they
    wasn't, he'd punish them twice over for being proud. He's been
    gone six hours. I ain't going to mind until it becomes absolutely
    necessary. I ought to put it off as long as possible. Each time,
    I ought to put it off a bit longer. Finally I'd give it up. Even if
    he never showed up all night, I'd remain in harmony with
    myself and with nature.
[*LIZ enters with a boiling kettle*]
LIZ: How can you sit there without your shoes on? The ants will get
    up your legs.
STEPHI: They can and welcome.
LIZ: What they do, they undermine the paving. They dig it out
    underneath. One day, it will simply tip down. [*She pours
    boiling water on the ground*] I don't like ants, I'm sorry to say.
STEPHI: It's so warm and peaceful, you didn't ought to kill them
    at a time like this.
LIZ: Ants don't stop for sentiment. If I was to do this every day for
    a year they'd still be marching up from under there. They don't
    all die at once. Sly creatures. [*Pours some more water*]
STEPHI: I thought you was an animal lover.
LIZ: To them that deserve it I am.

STEPHI: I'm glad you ain't God.

LIZ: If I was God, I'd make nicer insects.

[*JAMES comes in*]

JAMES: Anybody ask for me?

STEPHI: No.

JAMES: Anybody telephone?

STEPHI: No.

[*JAMES goes in, switches on the answering machine. A message from CELESTINE*]

CELESTINE: This fucking ansaphone. Where are you James? Just a minute while I light my cigarette. Shit. Nearly dropped the lighter in my lap. That would be a big mistake. It's that hot down there, it'd go up in flames. That ain't the reason I'm phoning. I seen Oliver. Oliver says he ain't got nothing for you because Richard, Terry and Patrick are all in custody. He don't want you coming round. I told him no way could you be to blame, all right? It's three o'clock in the morning and I wish you was here. If the wrong person hears this it's your own fucking fault. Answer the fucking phone next time.

JAMES: [*Switches off the machine and comes back into the yard*] What you looking at. [*Silence*] Did you know that was on there?

LIZ: No.

JAMES: Stupid time to phone.

LIZ: Did you shop them James?

JAMES: Is there anything to eat?

STEPHI: You germ.

JAMES: I'm sorry she phoned, all right. What am I supposed to do.

STEPHI: Did you shop them?

JAMES: What's it to you?

STEPHI: I'm interested to know what you're capable of.

JAMES: Interested.

STEPHI: Yes, you're the most interesting person I've ever met.

JAMES: You're far more interested in me than I am in you. But then, what's there to know about you?

STEPHI: Don't rack your brains.

JAMES: Do you think I feel jealous? I don't. That's how predictable you are. I see you with someone else, it don't bother me.

STEPHI: Good. I'll bear that in mind.

JAMES: Next time you're talking to your friend next door,

remember to thank him for destroying my credibility. I'm skint,
ain't I. I'm unemployed. I'm going to have to live off you
from now on, and you can't even afford to keep me in this
hairstyle. What you being so quiet for? Tired are you. You
ought to get a better job. Since you been out cleaning your
hands are like alligator paws. They ain't soft like they used to
be.

STEPHI: No. And they'll harden to stone and wear away to dust
before you'll speak to me kindly.

JAMES: This ain't the first time that things have gone wrong for
me. But I'm lucky. My enemies go down and I survive. You
want to know what I'm capable of. I'm capable of anything.
What you want me to do? You want a demonstration. What you
doing with the kettle, Liz? Give it here. Come on, give it, it
ain't yours. Now watch this, Steph. I'm going to throw it on
you, look. [*Makes as if to throw it. LIZ screams*] Don't you
trust me? What you take me for? You got a high opinion of me,
ain't you. I can't make you out. You're living every day with
someone who puts you in fear. It's unbalanced.

[*JOHN puts his head over the fence that divides his garden from
theirs*]

JAMES: What's your problem?

JOHN: I got no problem.

JAMES: You think so.

JOHN: Why did she scream?

JAMES: She's hungry.

JOHN: [*To STEPHI*] Is he threatening you?

JAMES: What's it to you?

JOHN: [*Climbs in over the fence as LIZ hurries out*] Be sensible.

JAMES: [*Taking out a knife, gripping JOHN and threatening him
with it*] You're trespassing.

JOHN: [*Alarmed*] The weak have recourse to weapons, but the
superior man uses no shield.

JAMES: You're an absolute dick.

JOHN: The strong man gives way when the weak are inflexible. The
weak not uncommonly appear to have the upper hand.

JAMES: You're an unbelievable arsehole.

JOHN: The strong understand the weak, the weak fail to understand
the strong. We come into this world looking for friends.

JAMES: Nobody wants to be your friend. You're like a newborn baby. You ought to be left outside to die. Nobody wants to change your nappy. Nobody wants to feed you. You got the brains of a calf. What you want a friend for? We're born alone and we die alone. Especially some.

[*LIZ returns with REG, SHEILA and MICHAEL*]

SHEILA: Summer at last. The great outdoors.

REG: Watch yourself James. If I was him I'd have had that knife off you by now.

[*JAMES looks at JOHN. REG disarms him*]

JAMES: You animal, you hurt my hand.

REG: I never even touched you. The man with the knife in his hand needs eyes in the four sides of his head, like the seraphim of the Old Testament.

LIZ: [*Conversationally, to JOHN*] I'm glad we weren't too late.

JAMES: What you all looking at? You know me, I like to fool about. I like a joke, don't I.

JOHN: You evil little cunt. You little twister.

REG: When we want your views we'll ask for them.

MICHAEL: But we ain't going to want them.

JOHN: One of you pissed through my door last night. What pervert done that?

MICHAEL: I never pissed through no fucking door.

JAMES: Nobody pissed through no fucking door. Somebody don't like you.

JOHN: Are you all in this? How can you stand for it? Aren't you ashamed? Yes, you're ashamed, and you don't like being ashamed, and you don't like being reminded you're ashamed, so you can't stand the sight of me. It's perfectly logical. Where will it end? Petrol through the door, put a match in. Ain't you got any pity? My mother hides in there all day, she puts her clothes on then she gets back into bed. She won't have the curtains open. It's like a fucking funeral parlour with her lying on her back in there. How many people are doing it? Is it two or three? Is it the whole street? I'm cut off and I'm shut in. I'm like a prisoner. The mind of the prisoner tries to travel out through the building, but it's too weak to reach the outside wall. All of a sudden it's as if he's in his tomb.

LIZ: I feel sick to my stomach.

SHEILA: She's too high strung, bless her.

MICHAEL: [*To LIZ*] Do you want a mint?

SHEILA: She ought to go inside.

LIZ: No I'll stay here if you don't mind. I'll have a mint.

REG: [*To JOHN*] You ain't doing no good here. There's nothing to be gained by histrionics.

JAMES: He's in my garden.

REG: [*To JOHN*] Take yourself off.

JOHN: What am I going to do?

JAMES: If you don't get off my premises I'm going to call the cops.

JOHN: Stephi? What am I going to do?

JAMES: Yeah. Ask her.

REG: A fair fight. Man to man and toe to the breadbasket. In mediaeval times, barehanded men could fight to the death. They weren't in such a hurry in those days.

SHEILA: I seen kangaroos do it on TV.

[*MARGARET appears at a window of her house, looking into the yard*]

MARGARET: Who's there, is it him? What's he doing there? I been looking up and down the house for you. Are you coming in now?

JOHN: In a minute.

MARGARET: Who's that you're talking to?

JOHN: You remember Stephi.

MARGARET: Hullo love. How you been keeping?

STEPHI: Well, thank you.

MARGARET: I ain't seen you, have I?

JOHN: You ain't been out.

MARGARET: I ain't been going about much. You better not ask me why. Don't want to tell the world, do I. You can't be too careful.

STEPHI: No.

MARGARET: I ain't been very well.

STEPHI: Ain't you?

MARGARET: I've had an accident. I must have been upset, mustn't I. I didn't know where he'd got to. I been trying to wipe it up. It's embarrassing, ain't it.

JAMES: [*Sotto voce*] So we'd best keep it to ourselves.

MARGARET: You don't mind, do you.

STEPHI: No.

MARGARET: I don't know what come over me. We've had some

trouble you know. You'd never believe what goes on, would you. There's people round here that are not quite human.

MICHAEL: [*Sotto voce*] That's cause they're muppets.

MARGARET: I'm sorry if I don't come down and meet your friends. I washed my things out. I got fresh on. He only needs to come and do the carpet.

JOHN: I'll be there in a minute.

MARGARET: I don't want it to smell.

STEPHI: No.

MARGARET: Good night, love. Nice talking to you.

STEPHI: Goodnight Margaret.

ALL: [*Except JOHN*] Goodnight Margaret. [*MARGARET goes*]

MICHAEL: Go and wipe it up John.

JAMES: You don't want it to smell.

MICHAEL: You ought to rub her nose in it, teach her not to do it again.

SHEILA: Shut it, Michael.

JOHN: [*To JAMES*] What do you want from me?

JAMES: I don't want nothing from you.

JOHN: I got to live. Ain't I?

JAMES: What you asking me for?

JOHN: Because I don't fucking know.

JAMES: Why don't you put it to the test. You know what I done once? I tried to hang myself off the branch of a tree, but it broke and I found myself sitting on the ground alive. Since then I got no worries. I made the offer but it wasn't accepted. I do what I like since then. I think I'm going to live to be a hundred. Have you got a head for spirits?

JOHN: No.

JAMES: I got a bottle of vodka in there. [*To LIZ*] Go and fetch it. [*She goes*] I believe in chance, it's what I live by. I respect it like a god. Most people hide from it, they build up a wall. They think, if they take care and lead a sensible life, they'll be spared. They get punished by chance for wanting to do a deal. [*LIZ reappears*] Some people can drink a bottle of vodka straight down, and they're laughing. Other people fall down dead.

JOHN: I'll drink it for this reason. I'll drink it to prove you can trust me.

JAMES: What you want me to trust you for? I don't trust nobody.

I don't trust myself.

JOHN: I'll drink it if it means you'll let me be.

JAMES: It ain't me. I got people that want to do things to please me.

JOHN: Would they stop then?

JAMES: They might.

JOHN: The man who drinks poison and lives becomes a superior man.

JAMES: Right then. [*Hands him the vodka*] Afterwards we'll bear no grudge.

JOHN: I'll drink to that. [*He drinks the whole bottle while the others watch*] Time to go home.

JAMES: Mind how you go.

[*JOHN goes out through the front of the house*]

JAMES: Stupid fucker. He done it. Did you see that? As obedient as a little child. I felt sorry for the poor bewildered cunt. I almost found myself saying, "look, John, you don't have to do this, we love you, course we do." I can't believe it. Eager. What a twat.

LIZ: It'll be on your conscience if that don't agree with him, won't it. You'll never live that down.

MICHAEL: Bollocks. It's euthanasia.

SHEILA: I got such a thirst on me. You got any more of them bottles, James? I could go a whole one and all.

STEPHI: Good-natured, ain't you Sheila. I've never seen you anything but good-natured. That's because you got the finer feelings of a fucking rhinoceros.

SHEILA: I thought you said you didn't fancy him.

REG: You and your friends been giving him a hard time, ain't you James. It's a shame, in my opinion, that you ain't a fighter.

JAMES: You split old punchbag. You moralizing lump of shit. You think I'm the son you never had, you bender. You always want to patronize me. You're always making out you understand me. You understand nothing about me. If you was to understand one fucking thing about me, that would be the thing I'd change. Because all a failure understands is failure. You failed thug. You're carved in concrete. I'd rather be dead. I can move, see. I can fly. You're slow. I'm quick. You're stiff. I'm flexible. You're limited. I'm unlimited. If you don't like what I done, why didn't you stop me. You was there. Not one of you raised your voice. I heard fuck-all of a fucking word from any of you.

LIZ: You've always had your own way.

JAMES: That's because I'm surrounded by weakness. One shake and you'd all fall off me like fleas.

SHEILA: Get us a drink Michael. I refuse to be slagged off any more unless I got a drink in my hand.

REG: [*To JAMES*] A man's honour was at stake. The onlookers' hands was tied.

STEPHI: [*To REG*] He don't mean it. He goes a bit mental. He needs loyalty.

REG: One day girl, I'll teach you what's needed and what ain't.

JAMES: [*To STEPHI*] I see you move your lips, but your voice comes out from between your fucking legs.

[*JOHN, already very drunk, appears at the fence*]

JOHN: No James, no mate, don't speak to her like that. You don't mean it. [*To STEPHI*] He don't mean it.

JAMES: Ain't you dead yet?

JOHN: No.

JAMES: Well fuck off and don't come back till you are.

JOHN: I come to tell you. I understood everything. I come through my front door and that vodka hit me. I was sitting down on the floor, and at that moment I understood everything. Everything. I can't remember it.

JAMES: What a shame.

JOHN: I was sitting there, not sad and not happy. Because emotion, what is it? Powerful engines were massaging the inside of my head. Engines or butterflies, powerful butterflies. The roar of their wings seemed to set me apart, on an island, and then I heard, very faintly, human voices. This reminded me of you. Because I'm fond of you. That's ridiculous, ain't it. How can this be? [*He climbs into the yard*] Everyone we know is part of us. You are part of me. I am part of you. [*He sits down, dropping his wallet out of his pocket. He picks it up, opens it, shows a picture to SHEILA*] Battersea Park.

SHEILA: Is it? Yes, I can see the grass. And the trees.

JOHN: [*Pointing to the photo*] Who's this then?

SHEILA: It's never you, is it?

JOHN: Who's that I'm with?

SHEILA: Your mum and dad, is it?

JOHN: My auntie.

SHEILA: [*Takes a closer look*] Let's see.

JOHN: She's dead.

SHEILA: She's never.

JOHN: Yes, unfortunately. She only took me there the once.

SHEILA: What was her name?

JOHN: Annie.

MICHAEL: Knock knock. Who's there. Annie. Annie who. Annie never went there again.

SHEILA: She wasn't Annie Palmer, was she?

JOHN: That's right.

SHEILA: You mean to say she's Annie Palmer?

JOHN: Yes.

SHEILA: My sister was a friend of Annie Palmer's cousin Linda. You remember Linda, Reg.

REG: She had a mole.

SHEILA: No she didn't, that was Elizabeth. Linda married the youngest Bodoni boy. There was three of them, Giulio, Maurizio and Terence.

MICHAEL: My dad had a partner Maurizio Bodoni.

SHEILA: He never, did he?

MICHAEL: He done a runner.

SHEILA: Well he would, wouldn't he. Too fast to live, he was. He would have whipped the rug from under a dervish. Did you ever hear what he done to Graham Frith?

MICHAEL: Who's Graham Frith.

LIZ: Graham Frith used to visit our mum.

SHEILA: Now ain't that extraordinary.

JAMES: Not really. Show me the man that didn't visit our mum.

SHEILA: It gives you a sense of a greater pattern. His wife was Jane. She used to be Jane Raynor.

[*MARGARET appears at the fence*]

MARGARET: Jane Raynor was half sister to my husband. Did you know Jane?

SHEILA: She was an angel.

MARGARET: She was a saint.

SHEILA: Couldn't do enough for you.

MARGARET: Nothing was ever a trouble.

SHEILA: Tragic, weren't it.

MARGARET: Oh, it were tragic.

SHEILA: Still, it was better really.

MARGARET: It were a mercy really.

SHEILA: Come round tomorrow love, eh? You know where I live don't you. Just the other side. John'll tell you. Come round in the morning, we can have a talk.

[*JOHN falls to the ground*]

SHEILA: Your boy's had a drink too many.

MARGARET: Always something, ain't there.

SHEILA: Don't worry, love, let him sleep it off.

MARGARET: No point in worrying. The doctor give me some pills to calm me down.

SHEILA: Lovely.

MARGARET: I ought to take one, oughtn't I.

SHEILA: You do what you want, bless you.

MARGARET: I'll go in and take one. Be seeing you then.

SHEILA: Churra, love.

[*REG has been looking at JOHN*]

REG: He's croaked.

JAMES: That's all I need.

REG: He's lost all his tone, see.

MICHAEL: I never seen a dead man before. Show us his eyes, Reg.

STEPHI: Why don't you get down and have a good look. Count his teeth while you're about it.

JAMES: What are we going to do?

REG: Get on the phone, Shiel, get a doctor.

SHEILA: What you want to drag me in for?

JAMES: What's a doctor going to do, vaccinate him?

REG: [*To SHEILA*] We knew about James.

SHEILA: Knowing is no reason to suffer.

JAMES: I want him shifted out of here.

SHEILA: We've done enough for you. We've made enough exceptions for you. Shame you never made no exception for us.

REG: He shouldn't have died.

JAMES: That's why you've got to help me.

SHEILA: We don't got to do anything. We deserved better from you. You owed it to us to keep us out of your childishness.

REG: He needn't have died. The odds were against it.

SHEILA: That's where James has let us down. That's his gratitude. I'm off.

STEPHI: I'm getting the doctor.

JAMES: Wait up. What you going to tell them?

REG: We felt no malice towards anyone. Therefore this shouldn't
    have happened.
SHEILA: Come on, or we'll be witnesses.
REG: Therefore we want no part of it.
[*They leave*]
JAMES: [*To STEPHI*] What you going to tell them?
LIZ: He looks so lifelike, don't he.
STEPHI: I'll say we was having a drink.
JAMES: Where are the glasses then? Get some glasses.
STEPHI: Stop acting like you killed him. [*She goes*]
MICHAEL: I got to take a video back. They'll be shutting up shop.
JAMES: Ain't you going to stay with me?
MICHAEL: We all got to stand on our own two feet some time.
JAMES: But Michael, this ain't the time.
MICHAEL: Your feet are out of my hands. [*He goes*]
LIZ: You never seem to keep your friends.
[*JAMES turns and hits her. She retreats into the house*]
JAMES: [*To the corpse*] Nobody cares you're dead. So don't come
    crying to me. You got your mouth jammed open. [*Attempts to
    shut it*] You're getting very cold. Look at that. You got one ear
    bigger than the other. [*Holds them both*] The left one is half as
    big again. It didn't notice, though. People don't look that close,
    do they. Not when you're alive. I could look at you all over,
    you wouldn't care now, would you. I'm sorry you're dead, all
    right. You'll hold this against me permanently, won't you. I got
    a stomach ache. You're giving me a stomach ache. I ought to
    have kept my distance.
JOHN'S VOICE: Are you sorry then?
JAMES: Don't make out you're talking to me. I ain't a madman.
JOHN'S VOICE: But I am talking to you, you can hear me clear as
    a bell.
JAMES: I ain't listening. I can't hear nothing, all right? It's very
    quiet, actually, tonight. I can hear them washing up five doors
    away.
JOHN'S VOICE: Yes, it's a nice night.
JAMES: Don't speak to me, fuck you. Get away.
JOHN'S VOICE: I can't.
JAMES: Yes you can. I'm going to help you. I'm going to sit here,
    very quiet, and relax my body, first the feet and legs, then
    working my way up until I reach the hair of my head. When

I'm completely relaxed, you will disengage.

JOHN'S VOICE: You think you're in control, but you ain't. I died without anybody crying for me. I'm lonely. I never set out to be your enemy. I wanted to be your friend. I wasn't good enough, was I.

JAMES: You want me to apologize, I'll apologize. I'm sorry I had that attitude.

[*STEPHI comes out into the yard*]

STEPHI: Who you talking to?

JOHN'S VOICE: Tell her.

JAMES: [*Furtive*] No, get fucked.

STEPHI: James?

JAMES: Did you get through to the doctor?

STEPHI: They'll call back.

JOHN'S VOICE: Typical. Just as well I ain't dying.

JAMES: What do you expect? The surgery's closed.

JOHN'S VOICE AND STEPHI: That's when these things always happen.

JAMES: Eh?

STEPHI: Are you all right?

JOHN'S VOICE: Tell her, tell her.

JAMES: Why shouldn't I be?

JOHN'S VOICE: Don't try to pretend I don't exist.

JAMES: Shut it or you'll get me put away.

STEPHI: What you think I am.

JAMES: Not you for fuck's sake.

JOHN'S VOICE: Tell her.

STEPHI: You're upset. You don't need to fight it. It means you're good if you're upset. It means you're sorry. That why I would never betray you, because you're good.

JOHN'S VOICE: You and I know better, don't we.

JAMES: [*Kicks JOHN's corpse*] Stupid wanker.

STEPHI: James!

JAMES: Fuck off! [*To JOHN's corpse*] Taking liberties are you? Think you're special because you're fucking dead. [*Kicks and attacks JOHN's corpse. STEPHI runs off*] Think you've finally cracked it. This is what I think of you. You're a loser. The eternal fucking loser. [*Stands exhausted. Silence*] He's fucked off. I thought he'd never take the hint. That would be the end, I mean it. I wouldn't go through life with him dossing about in my brain like he was in bed up there. I'd top myself rather than put up with that. I do let some of them in. If they're kind and want to tell me things I need to know. I never used to get them, they waited till I was ready, and then they come and told me about the people of the future, that will survive when the rest can't breathe in the air any more. Because the world is rotten. The people of the future will look like anybody else but they got a second way of breathing. When the air finally goes black and the world is like a festering sore, the second breathers will be the only ones left, because they can breathe poison and thrive on it like the sweetest air. I been told this because I'm a second breather. They come and tell me things to my advantage. And if I get the other kind, that only want to rubbish me and take away my secrets, I don't let them in. I'm always in control of what gets talked about in my mind and of who's listening. That's why if Stephi ever starts in about me needing the doctor I know for a fact she's talking bollocks. It's getting cooler now. I feel cool.

JOHN'S VOICE: You're a cunt, James. You treated me like a cunt.

JAMES: Ah. God.

JOHN'S VOICE: I was weak and helpless. I was unwanted. You'd do anything rather than be like that.

JAMES: God won't you fuck off.

JOHN'S VOICE: It's your greatest fear. Why did you choose that fear? Because it's your destiny.

JAMES: Bollocks.

JOHN'S VOICE: Why is it your destiny? Because you're different. You're heartless. Who wants you, James? Weak people want you, people you can fool. There's nothing to you. You're empty inside.

JAMES: I ain't listening to you.

JOHN'S VOICE: When people find you out, you'll be left to perish. You're weak. That's why you can hear me. You ain't got the inner strength.

JAMES: Try me.

JOHN'S VOICE: I will try you. I'll always try you. Just wait till people start to hear you answering me back. Stephi's probably on the phone right now, phoning for the doctor.

JAMES: Don't give me that bullshit.

JOHN'S VOICE: Lie down, James.

JAMES: Get stuffed.

JOHN'S VOICE: It's a hard world for a weak boy. Always fighting, always pretending. No-one loves you because no-one knows you. And if they did know you, they wouldn't love you. Because you don't deserve it. Lie down with me, I'm the one that understands you.

JAMES: Never.

JOHN'S VOICE: Lie down. It's natural. You been under a lot of pressure. Lie down close to me and I won't talk. I'll let you alone.

JAMES: You won't talk.

JOHN'S VOICE: I'll give you a break. I'm sorry for you. You never was sorry for me.

JAMES: You swear you won't talk.

JOHN'S VOICE: I swear.

JAMES: I'll lie down for a bit.

JOHN'S VOICE: Clear your head.

JAMES: I'll lie down.

JOHN'S VOICE: We'll be company for each other.

[*JAMES lies down. MARGARET appears at a window*]

MARGARET: What they doing down there. I wouldn't lay down there. They'll catch their death. Everything to live for, and all they can do is lay about down there. John? Are you coming in?

THE END